Ted Bundy

The Horrific True Story Behind America's
Most Wicked Serial Killer

Real Crime by Real Killers Volume 4

Second Edition

Ryan Becker, True Crime Seven

TRUE CRIME 7

Table of Contents

Explore the Stories of

The Murderous Minds

A Note

From True Crime Seven

Hi there!

Thank you so much for picking up our book! Before you continue your exploration into the dark world of killers, we wanted to take a quick moment to explain the purpose of our books.

Our goal is to simply explore and tell the stories of various killers in the world: from unknown murderers to infamous serial killers. Our books are designed to be short and inclusive; we want to tell a good scary true story that anyone can enjoy regardless of their reading level.

That is why you won't see too many fancy words or complicated sentence structures in our books. Also, to prevent the typical cut and dry style of true crime books, we try to keep the narrative easy to follow while incorporating fiction style storytelling. As to information, we often find ourselves with too little or too much. So, in terms of research material and content, we always try to include what further helps the story of the killer.

Lastly, we want to acknowledge that, much like history, true crime is a subject that can often be interpreted differently. Depending on the topic and your upbringing, you might agree or disagree with how we present a story. We understand disagreements are inevitable. That is why we added this note so hopefully, it can help you better understand our position and goal.

Now without further ado, let the exploration to the dark begin!

Introduction

WHEN WE ARE CHILDREN, WE SPEND OUR TIME watching cartoons or reading tales that make an effort of stressing the great duality of good and evil, mostly in a clichéd manner. We learn to spot the good guys—those handsome people with friendly smiles and helpful manners; while the bad guys are always quick to grin, appear ambitious, and openly cruel human beings that regularly reveal their intentions early into the story.

However, in real life, things are often not this easy. History has taught us that some of the despicable, merciless, and bloodthirsty monsters have typically been those people who demonstrated the behavior that we falsely believed to be signs of *'goodness'*; purposely used to manipulate their victims and lull them into a false sense of security.

11

Ted Bundy was one such man—best-known for doing this, in fact—a killer who was as friendly as he was seductive. A heartless and remorseless murderer, Bundy overpowered and desecrated his victims' bodies—both before and after death. Their corpses were his playthings until they rotted and he had to dispose of them.

Quite possibly the most famous American serial killer alongside Jeffrey Dahmer, Bundy's name spread terror across the United States during the 1970s, while his killing and raping spree alone qualified this title, he can also claim two successful prison escapes that had women all around the nation terrified to go out at night.

Was he prolific? Yes, very much so—he confessed to killing well over thirty women, but it is believed that he killed many more. *Were his crimes widespread?* Scarily, yes. Women in up to seven states were his targets, and he would have gone on for longer if he had not been stopped.

Bundy was a natural-born killer who lived to cause pain, and you, the reader, are about to find out just how terrible the man was.

Ted, the main protagonist of our book, became known as The Campus Killer, as well as many other identities he adopted during his time evading law enforcement. This book will provide you with explicit details of his life and his killings. Murders, rapes, dismemberments, Bundy was a man who "did it all," and these events have been researched for your interest or disgust, depending on its relevancy.

As you will see, the ugly parts have not been toned down, nor is any of the gruesomeness that sensitive readers may have wished to avoid reading, been eliminated. So be warned…

…The horror that was Ted Bundy is about to begin.

I

The Birth of a Psychopath

EVERY MONSTER BORN INTO THE WORLD IS AN innocent, screaming baby—Ted Bundy was no exception. On November 24th, 1946, our killer was born Theodore Robert to Louise Cowell in the city of Burlington, Vermont. In regards to his father, nothing certain can be said—it has never been determined, despite Louise claiming on the boy's birth certificate the father had been a salesman and Air Force veteran. There were rumors among the family that Louise's own dad may have fathered the child, but no evidence was ever produced supporting this claim.

Whichever the case, Louise moved into her parent's house with the newborn Ted, and lived in Samuel and Eleanor Powell's home for three years. During this time, they began feeding Ted a lie—one he wouldn't know the truth of for many years—primarily due to social stigma and old-fashioned beliefs. The trio of adults agreed to make everyone believe Ted had been born to Samuel and Eleanor, and that his mother Louise was his older sister. These lies would go on until Ted reached his college years; the rage of being lied to for so long may have contributed to developing his psychopathic disorders.

Within the Powell household, Samuel was an abusive tyrant. In spite of initial claims that Ted had been close and looked up to the man, his family would later admit the grandparent had been extremely violent, bigoted, and regularly spoke to himself. Bullying at home was so powerful that Eleanor aged into a depressive, withdrawn, old woman who required periodical electroconvulsive therapy to treat her mental state.

Young Theodore watched this all through confused, infant eyes and it definitely affected him. At one point, he surrounded his aunt Julia with kitchen knives while she was sleeping. Then he stood by her with a grin until she awoke. While this is a disturbing behavior for any child, the fact that Ted was only three years old when it occurred, made it that more disturbing.

When Ted was four, Louise decided to move to Tacoma, Washington, where her cousins, Alan and Jane Scott, lived. This would be where Ted's young life would develop and his first run-ins with the law would occur; although they were minor offenses and showed no sign of a soon-to-be serial rapist and killer.

A year after the move to Washington, Louise met a hospital cook at church and they instantly fell for each other. The man, Johnny Culpepper Bundy, formally adopted Ted as his son, soon going on to have four children with Louise. Ted was always distant, feeling uncomfortable around Johnny and the children, and would state later that he had never liked him.

Ted's own recollections of his teenage life were memories of reading crime novels and magazines for stories and scenes that included sexual violence and maimed bodies, as well as peeping in women's bedroom windows. Ted's mother would claim he was an excellent son who never forgot a special occasion to gift her with something; he often spoke of his dream to be a policeman or a lawyer. Classmates also remembered Ted as a friendly, well-known student, yet Bundy claimed to biographers he had never grasped the concept of friendship.

Ted Bundy's behavior soon showed sociopathic signs and a general disregard for the law. Breaking into cars, Ted would steal objects he found inside with the intent of selling them. He was also quite skilled at shoplifting, taking advantage of it to support his skiing hobby. Ted was arrested, at least twice as a minor; however, the details of the incidents were expunged from his record as soon as he reached the age of eighteen.

Ted was done with high school by 1965 and began studying at the University of Puget Sound. He did not like it there because his classmates were all from wealthy backgrounds and it made him feel inferior. After a year, he transferred to the University of Washington, where he studied Chinese. At the same time, he looked for simple, minimum wage jobs; he never lasted longer than a few months at a time. Whether it was working as a grocery bagger, shelf-stocker, or volunteer at a Seattle suicide hotline, his superiors remembered him as an unreliable and untrustworthy young man. Ted also volunteered in political activities for the Republican Party, such as Nelson Rockefeller's presidential campaign of 1968.

It was around this time that Ted met the woman that would perhaps become the most pivotal of his life, even more so than any of his unfortunate victims. Although he had never been a model boy, things were about to turn a lot uglier in Ted's young life.

II

The Grudge

T ED HAD A PROBLEM THAT HAD BEEN tormenting him all his life.

He always wanted to be just like those wealthy, happy young men he had studied with at both universities. Part of that was finding a beautiful girlfriend he could parade around, who would give him the support he craved. Ted finally found her in the spring of 1967, a beautiful young woman named Stephanie Brooks. She was pretty, rich, smart, and had a lot of class, just like the women he had observed longingly at university. Just like Ted, Stephanie studied at the University of Washington. She also loved him a lot.

Ted was truly happy around Stephanie; he envisioned a future where the two could be married and grow old together. However, while he was picturing these things, Stephanie was growing increasingly uncomfortable with her boyfriend's lack of ambition in life. He did not seem to be on a path to success. Her parents also appeared to dislike her partner, and this may have been an influence on the decision she took next.

When Stephanie told Ted of her decision to break up with him, he was in shock. It was a slap in the face for someone he had been trying so hard to impress, and find a way to be like the rich boys he envied. Despite many letters and attempts at recovering the relationship, Ted was unable to accomplish anything and it got to him. He entered a depressive stage, filled with rage and confusion, which led to dark thoughts.

Ted's heart was broken, and he began to harbor a deep hatred toward women—most of the victims whose lives he took were women that looked very similar to Stephanie: Caucasian, dark-haired, and beautiful.

It was around this time, in early 1969, that Bundy traveled east and visited several relatives in Arkansas and Philadelphia. He went in search of his origins and discovered birth records in Burlington,

Vermont, revealing the true details of his birth and parentage. This did not help his state of mind, furthering his anger toward the world.

He returned to Washington later that same year and met Elizabeth Kloepfer—known as Meg Anders in some documentation. She was a divorcée and single mother from Ogden, Utah, working as a secretary at the university. Elizabeth became Ted's next girlfriend, though he was not faithful to her. Ted's life was about to take a change for the better...at least for now.

Back in Washington, Ted felt he had a chance to try again and he re-enrolled at the university, this time studying Psychology. His grades were excellent; he also had a good relationship with his professors and became friends with many people in various positions. One of those people was a writer named Ann Rule. She would go on to write one of Bundy's most well-known biographies, *The Stranger Beside Me.* Even though Ann believed Ted to be a sadistic sociopath, she took somewhat of a human, defensive stance on him. During this time, Ted also became interested in fulfilling his childhood wish of studying law and began to think of a school where he could study to become a lawyer.

Describing Ted's sexual habits, Meg Anders stated Ted was insistent on practicing sadomasochistic sexual intercourse with her, almost strangling her to unconsciousness, on one occasion, despite her pleas for him to stop. He also requested she remain completely still when they had sex, not making a sound as if she was a corpse. Only in this manner could Ted reach orgasm.

Bundy graduated in 1972, and immediately joined Governor Daniel J. Evans' re-election campaign. He had started sending admission requests to begin his studies at several law schools, and some were considering giving him a chance. Ted stated that in his eyes, the law was the answer to his search for order. During his time working for Governor Evans, he followed Evans' opponent Albert Rosellini around, recording his speeches for analysis. Evans was successfully re-elected and Bundy caught the attention of Ross Davis, Chairman of the Washington State Republican Party. The chairman liked Ted and the way he worked and helped him with recommendations. These ended up helping Ted get accepted by both University of Puget Sound and University of Utah's law schools in early 1973, despite that he had not done well in the admission tests. He would decide on University of Puget Sound law school the following year.

Ted Bundy was on the rise. His success was spreading and he was showing signs of being a truly heroic citizen—on one occasion, he saved a three-year-old child from drowning and was rewarded with a medal by the city's police department. On another occasion, he was involved in performing a citizen's arrest on a thief who attempted to steal a person's bag. Bundy recovered the bag and gave it back to its rightful owner—an act that did not go unnoticed.

On a revisit to the University of Washington's campus, Ted came across his friends and professors; everyone had something positive to say about him. His newfound security and position in society were highly respected by his peers and teachers, and they now had a far different—and better—image of him than before.

Despite all the success and good news, Ted would get another chance to feel triumphant.

One of Ted's business trips in the summer of 1973 took him to California, where he met up with Stephanie Brooks; at this point, he was still in a relationship with Meg Anders. Stephanie was shocked by Ted's transformation—he had gone from a man with no ambition and little vision to a successful politician, graduate, and now a law student. He was everything she had wished for in a man, and this made her re-start their relationship once more, primarily due to the fact that she did not know he was already with somebody else. Stephanie flew to Seattle to stay with him a few times, and Bundy even introduced her to his boss, Ross Davis, as his fiancée. They discussed marriage during this period, and Brooks was over the moon.

But it was all for nothing.

In January 1974, only a few months later, Ted stopped answering her calls and ignored her letters. He did not visit her anymore, nor did he seem interested in continuing a relationship with her. When she finally got a hold of him a month later and asked him why he had distanced himself without any explanation, he told her he had no idea what she meant and hung up. She never heard from him again.

Ted had achieved vengeance for her earlier breakup, and proved that he could have been her husband; the husband she had always wanted.

Ted Bundy would not be satisfied with what he had done to get his revenge on Stephanie. For some reason, it just was not enough. Perhaps he should have just let it all go—acknowledge things do not always go the way one wants them to go, and had taught Stephanie a lesson for rejecting him. Perhaps his inferiority complex had come back with added poison and started to eat at him and fill him with doubts. Maybe Ted simply wanted to hurt someone for the bad things that had happened to him.

Ted was about to pursue a new career, one much darker than any previous.

The rapes and murders were about to begin, and once they began, nobody could stop them…

…Well, not until it was too late.

III

Something Finally Snaps

IT HAD BEEN A GOOD PERIOD FOR TED. ONE THAT had given him hope, showing him he was somebody worth a damn and could make a difference in the world. He had given his life a massive turn for the better, and rubbing shoulders with some pretty influential men and women.

Curiously, Ted's participation in the Republican Party would bring him close to Rosalynn Carter, President Jimmy Carter's wife, who in turn would have the strange misfortune of meeting John Wayne 'Killer Clown' Gacy, and James 'Jim' Warren Jones; both infamous killers who were as scary as the protagonist of this biography.

Ted was troubled and spiteful toward women, with a strong fetish toward hardcore pornography involving rape, torture, and snuff. Speculation was he had acquired the taste for it from his grandfather, Samuel, who was believed to collect pornographic material of extremely violent content. This would define Ted, in spite of doing well in other aspects of his life.

The exact date and location of Bundy's first murder have never been confirmed, due to the fact that he has provided biographers and investigators with many different and conflicting accounts of his acts during the period of his first murder.

To this day, details are still not clear. Ted once confessed to a member of his defense team, Polly Nelson, whose career would arguably be destroyed by defending the monster that was Ted Bundy that he first attempted to kidnap a victim in 1969, on a visit to Ocean City, New Jersey. He also told her he committed his first murder in 1971.

However, he also told a psychologist he had killed two women in 1969 in Atlantic City but also confessed to a homicide detective that he had first murdered in Seattle in 1972, before taking another life in Washington in 1973.

The facts were even more confusing when evidence was found linking Ted to the 1961 abduction and murder of an eight-year-old in Tacoma; when he was fourteen. He denied it.

The truth is that while Ted Bundy's official murder/rape records may have started in January 1974, with his first sexual assault and attempted murder, his taste for causing pain started slowly and with small but telling signs manifesting themselves a few years before then.

In 1972, a woman recalled having sex with him during a one-night stand, in which Ted choked her almost into unconsciousness until he reached orgasm. When she confronted him on why he had done it, he feigned ignorance. He confessed regularly practicing the same act on other women, and that it would help him enter a new state of mind, giving him great pleasure.

Shortly after this event, Bundy stalked an attractive woman at a bar and followed her into a dark alley. There, he found a large plank of wood and advanced past her, expecting the woman to pass through a secluded area where he would ambush her. Nevertheless, the plan failed when the woman entered a nearby home. This attempted assault whetted his appetite for a future attack. He began to stalk other women in the hopes of getting a chance to rape and murder them.

Ted's first true attack occurred when he approached one of his stalking victims undetected, to the point he was literally right behind her. He carried a club and his victim was distracted, opening the front door to her home. Pouncing on her, Ted smacked her with the club, causing her to fall to the ground and scream out; at the last minute, he had second thoughts and fled the scene.

Ted was learning, perfecting his abilities, and honing the necessary skills he would use in the future. He was very diligent about leaving as little incriminating evidence at a crime scene as possible, as well as beginning to find ways to earn the trust of his victims. Everything was a soft set of practice attacks, eventually leading to the big moment of his first sexual assault.

It took place on January 4th, 1974.

Karen Sparks was an eighteen-year-old dancer who studied at the University of Washington. She lived alone in a basement apartment in Washington and never could have imagined what was going to happen to her on that cold night: literally ruining her life.

Ted had been stalking Karen and realizing she was all alone, broke into her apartment shortly after midnight through a window without waking her, and found her asleep. What he did next was horrific—he wrenched a metal rod from Karen's bed frame and used it to bludgeon her unconscious, repeatedly slamming it on her skull without mercy. When she had been knocked senseless, he took the same bloody rod and shoved it up her vagina, brutally assaulting her with the rod, causing extensive internal damage. Leaving her for dead, Ted disappeared into the night, but Karen survived and was found lying in a pool of her blood the next day. She entered a coma that would last several months. She survived the ordeal, but with permanent brain damage.

Bundy did not wait long for his next attack, either—this new assault ended in the death of his victim. It left such a mark on his mind, Bundy needed a period of recuperation.

In the early morning hours of February 1st, Bundy targeted a similar victim to the previous one; Lynda Ann Healy, a beautiful twenty-one-year-old Psychology student at the University of Washington, who worked with special-needs children. She also worked at a local radio station giving ski reports. Lynda had actually attended psychology classes with Bundy. She did not live alone, sharing her cozy 5517 Northeast 12th street residence with four other women.

Unfortunately, this fact did nothing to stop what happened to her. Lynda slept in the basement, while her best friend slept in the room beside her. The other three women slept on the floors above; all of the girls were quite close to one another.

The night before the attack, Ellie—Lynda's best friend and roommate—thought she saw a shadow move past the window on the side of the house. Although it put her on edge, she thought nothing more of it after noticing how the strong wind was pulling at the tree branches outside. The truth would never be known. In all likelihood, it was Ted Bundy, already planning what would take place the next morning.

It was a swift, ruthless attack. In spite of the girls' security awareness, one of the house doors had been left unlocked. This costly error allowed Bundy entry into the house, and he descended to the basement. The noise of his victim could be muffled by walls and ceilings. Unfortunately, his crime was a complete success. Lynda did not even realize Bundy was in the room and suffered a heavy blow, knocking her out instantly. Bundy then gagged her and removed her nightgown, taking a moment to dress her in jeans, a white blouse, and shoes.

Never directly admitting to killing Lynda, Bundy only hinted at what he *would have done* if he had abducted her—but it is believed he took Lynda to his home and kept her there, continuously raping and hurting her until she either died or he decided to kill her. Meanwhile, back at Lynda's home, three of the girls had early classes or jobs and had already left.

Ellie awoke to the sound of the phone ringing. It was Lynda's boss, asking why Lynda had not shown up for her daily report. This seemed very strange to Ellie; Lynda had mentioned meeting an ex-boyfriend that weekend, but she was always responsible with her job and classes. Ultimately, Ellie decided to continue getting ready for class and, for a few hours, forgot about her roommate's strange disappearance.

By nightfall, the girls would learn more information—a missing person report had been filed and two officers had visited the home to check for any suspicious signs, without success. However, lifting Lynda's bedsheets, one of her roommates found a large stain of dried blood on the pillow and mattress. A careful search of the room also revealed: a bloodstained nightgown and the discovery of missing clothes. The details began to reveal a story about what had taken place; someone made their way into the house, attacked Lynda, and carried her off.

The police, accompanied by Lynda's roommates and friends, fanned out to search for Lynda across the city and surrounding areas, as well as to question neighbors for any eyewitnesses. Both the searches and the questionings yielded nothing, and the girls of 5517 Northeast 12th street slowly lost hope in finding her again. It would not be until 1975, when Lynda's skull was discovered in a wooded location west of Seattle, resting in the dirt alongside the remains of five other victims, that Lynda's fate was revealed.

At first, the abduction of Lynda Healy was not associated with the work of a serial killer, but as more women began to disappear in the area, the general climate of terror started to grow.

Unfortunately, Ted Bundy was just getting started.

IV

Unleash the Beast

THE BRUTAL RAPE OF YOUNG KAREN SPARKS AND the murder of Lynda Ann Healy set off something within Ted Bundy's mind that would be difficult to stop; it was a hunger that would never be satisfied and a thirst which would never be sated. The demon within Ted Bundy's heart was fully awake, and only death would bring it to heel.

The rumors soon began: a killer was out there—a man who hunted young female students, doing horrible things to them. Ted would become the scourge of the city of Washington, and labeled the Campus Killer.

But not yet, however. For now, Ted Bundy's name was not even whispered in the dark. He was still the nice, charming man who had majored in Psychology and begun law school. Bundy stopped attending entirely in 1974 and worked alongside some of the biggest Republicans in the business. Ted remained a nice guy—nobody ever imagining he could turn out to be one of the most despicable American serial killers to have ever lived.

At this point in time, Bundy was no longer interested in home invasions and killing his victims where they lived. His modus operandi was evolving—he found it easier and smarter to take his victims away from lonely areas on the streets of the city, where he would not have to worry about witnesses, spotting him breaking-in or leaving victims' homes.

It was in this manner that another woman disappeared on March 12th. Donna Gail Manson, a nineteen-year-old student at the Evergreen State College in Olympia, disappeared without a trace. She set off one night on foot to attend a campus jazz concert but never arrived.

A month later, two female students from the same campus reported the suspicious presence of a man wearing an arm sling, on one occasion, and on another occasion using crutches. He asked the girls for help putting a pile of books in his vehicle—a Volkswagen Beetle. Both attempts failed when the women became suspicious after he insisted that they enter the car. Ted quickly left. The arm sling and other similar tricks rapidly became Bundy's best bet at capturing his victims; he worked on their pity and generosity to lure them, and then they were his.

Unfortunately, Ted's trick worked on Biology student Susan Rancourt, who was heading back to her dorm from an advisers' meeting at Central Washington State College; now Central Washington University. Bundy savagely hit her with a blunt object, proceeding to kidnap, rape, and murder her, then discarding her body alongside Lynda Healy's on a wooded incline.

On May 6th, just three weeks later and two hundred and sixty miles away from his hometown, Ted Bundy murdered once more. Roberta Kathleen Parks, a student of Religious Studies at Oregon State University, left her dormitory to go have a coffee with her best friends in the nearby College Union Building. However, she never arrived at her destination. Bundy approached and lured Roberta into his car, quickly driving further from the college and terrifying her into doing whatever he wanted. Stopping in a secluded area, Ted raped Roberta, returning afterward to Seattle, raping her again before murdering her and discarding her body.

The abduction of Roberta really put law enforcement on edge. Both the King's County Sheriff's Office and the Seattle Police Department began to increase efforts to find links and evidence that could lead them to the killer. All of the young women shared certain characteristics; they were all young, white, attractive college students with long hair, typically brunette, and parted in the middle. Rewards were offered for any information on the missing women, and eyewitnesses were encouraged to come forward and provide their recollections.

May turned into June, and with it came yet another victim. Bundy was no fool; he had followed the terror in the media and the details of the police investigation taking place in an attempt to stop him. By now, he knew people were keeping an eye out for a man asking for help or otherwise approaching women on the street. Therefore, he decided to slightly change his modus operandi and sate his bloodlust with someone willingly becoming his victim, without the trouble of having to kidnap her. His next murder would differ significantly in the way it took place, and Ted confessed he enjoyed it a lot.

Brenda Ball, a beautiful twenty-three-year-old woman, went alone to the Flame Tavern in the working-class neighborhood of Burien, Washington. She told friends she was going to try getting a ride to Sun Lakes, on the east side of the state, to meet them later and hang out. Yet, after asking a band member for a ride to the club, she might not be so lucky. All alone and with no way to get out to the club, a man approached and began to speak with her. With a sling on his arm and a charming smile on his face, Ted offered to take her home but invited her to a party beforehand, for which she accepted. One thing led to another, and the two had consensual sex—with Bundy unsuccessfully attempting to satisfy his extreme desires. Sadly, not long after, the demon within him whispered enticing words and Ted Bundy acted. He served Brenda enough alcohol to knock her into a state of stupor, raped her, finally strangling her to death.

After Brenda was dead, Bundy kept her body in his apartment for several days, constantly switching her from his bed to his wardrobe and vice-versa. He stated he no longer felt the urgency of getting rid of the body since he was in a private place; he had taken Brenda there without worrying about eyewitnesses spotting suspicious behavior. While at his home, Brenda's body was bathed and make-up applied to her face, before Ted finally tired of it and decapitated her. Her skull and mandible were found in the area around Taylor Mountain, Seattle. Her body's location was never discovered.

Only two weeks later, on the night of June 11th, 1974, Bundy returned to abduct another University of Washington victim from the campus. This time, Georgeann Hawkins, a popular and friendly eighteen-year-old student, avid swimmer and one who loved posing in front of a camera, was Bundy's choice. Georgeann had just said goodbye to her boyfriend at his dorm and began walking back to her own sorority house. A few hundred feet of brightly-lit alley separating both places was enough for Bundy to strike. As soon as the worried call from the sorority sisters arrived at Georgeann's parents' home, they knew their daughter was in trouble. She had no reason to run away and her relationship with friends was healthy.

Georgeann's body was never found, despite detectives carefully combing the alley the next morning. Eyewitnesses who were questioned afterward recalled seeing a man with a plastered leg and crutches in the area, struggling to carry a briefcase. Additionally, they claimed a woman helped him carry the case to his car, a light brown Volkswagen Beetle. Though she had not realized it, Georgeann had been in the presence of a serial killer.

Bundy returned to work as if nothing happened. He had found a job at the Washington State Department of Emergency Services in Olympia. Curiously, this agency was involved in the search of the missing women. Working there helped him keep an eye on what information law enforcement was gathering. While there, he met Carole Ann Boone, a divorced mother of two that would begin a relationship with Bundy in the future.

When links from the cases began to crisscross and meet, news about Bundy's crimes spread like wildfire—six women of similar characteristics missing, while another had been beaten savagely and raped. The states of Washington and Oregon were terrified of the crime; young women stopped hitch-hiking, or going to bars or other night-time activities. Law enforcement agencies had a real problem on their hands; the killer was smart enough to avoid leaving any physical evidence behind from the abductions, and forthcoming eyewitnesses provided little in terms of useful information.

Nonetheless, a certain pattern was definitely evolving. A sequence of details began creating a level of confidence among law enforcement officers, raising the hopes they had a chance of narrowing down their suspects and perhaps even capturing the man behind all this craziness. The women were all assaulted or taken at night, typically around construction sites and around the time of mid-term or final exams. Further, at most scenes, eyewitnesses had spotted a man wearing a cast or sling, and driving a brown or tan Volkswagen Beetle. It was just a matter of looking for the car, or having officers at the right place at the right moment—surely it should not be so difficult to catch the killer.

But unfortunately, things would not go as planned for law enforcement or for anyone who had expected to stop Ted Bundy. Women were still disappearing.

If anything, Ted Bundy had only just begun his spree. Soon, the police learned how big a mistake it was to underestimate Theodore Bundy.

V

Excelling at the Game

LTHOUGH HE WAS UNAWARE AT THE TIME, TED Bundy was about to conclude his killing spree in the Pacific Northwest. He was soon to leave the state of Washington for Utah, where he would receive an acceptance from the University of Utah's law school, and get a second chance at becoming a lawyer like he had dreamed of since childhood.

Having already abducted and killed half a dozen women, Ted did not want the number to remain at six. Six was too small a number for Ted—who had always been so ambitious and so indulging of his desires. He needed more.

Growing arrogant and full of himself, Ted's belief that he would not get caught, reflected what most serial killers end up thinking. He knew the police were after him and were just waiting for a moment to catch him at night. *So why not attack during the day?* It was a risk, but he was all about risks, putting effort into getting the prize at the end of it all. *Why stop at one victim in a single day? Why not two?* His next murders were going to be the most daring yet.

It was a bright, Sunday morning on June 14th, in the summer of 1974. Lake Sammamish's beach was crowded with families, and young men and women were bathing in the cool waters and enjoying a peaceful day. With an extremely hot morning and noon, a swim would definitely help out with lowering body temperatures and getting a beautiful tan while they were at it.

A group of young women was on the beach that day in their bathing suits—the feelings of summer joy in their hearts, taking in the sights, sounds, and smells of a lovely day…unaware a ruthless serial killer was observing them, while in a state of increasing agitation at the thought of finding a fresh victim. He was going to spill blood and fulfill his fantasies once more; it was only a matter of time, and Ted knew it.

At eleven-thirty in the morning, Ted Bundy headed out to the beach. He spotted Janice Graham, a blonde, twenty-two-year-old woman. A friendly voice spoke to her in a British or Canadian accent, saying a simple, "Hello." Before her stood a man in his mid-twenties, wearing a white tennis outfit, with his arm in a sling. He introduced himself as Ted and explained that he needed to load his sailboat on to his car, but was unable alone. He said this with a smile, pointing to his sling.

Janice felt awkward denying Ted help and followed him to the boat. They set off for the parking lot just off the beach. He spoke to her as they walked, making small talk and wincing in pain as he moved his arm. Janice did not find him suspicious in the slightest and had probably not heard of the previous disappearances; she answered his questions and revealed that she lived in the nearby city of Bellevue.

The conversation made their walk seem shorter, and before Janice knew it, she was standing by a metallic brown, 'newish-looking' Volkswagen Beetle. Her smile died and an alarm bell rang in her head. There was no sailboat, and the parking lot was emptier than the beach had been. When she asked what was going on, Ted dismissed her worries and told her the sailboat was nearby, up the road at his parent's house. All her pretenses of trusting and helping him ended at that moment and she conveniently remembered she had to meet her loved ones.

Ted reacted pleasantly to the rejection and let her go with a smile, soon returning to the beach to look for someone else who could help him. Janice would recall seeing him heading back in the direction of the parking lot and laughed at how *good* he was at what he did. Much later, she realized who she had interacted with.

Ironically, a second Janice enters this story; however, her fate not as fortunate as Janice Graham. Janice Ott was twenty-three, short, thin, and blonde, who, like Bundy himself, had studied psychology and worked as a probation officer in Seattle. She was a warm-hearted young woman who believed in helping those in need. She had a wonderful personality and was loved by her fellow co-workers and her husband of one year, who studied medicine in California. Janice Ott headed down to the beach on her own that day, grabbing her bike and leaving a note for her roommate she was going to spend a day tanning under the sun.

Bundy was standing just off the beach, watching all the girls—as a male eyewitness and DEA agent—would recall later. Ted seemingly discarded most of the women at the beach until he spotted Ott lying on the beach and walked toward her. He did not take long to repeat the same process he had used on the first Janice: asking her to help him load his sailboat on to his car. Janice Ott was certainly more flirtatious than Janice Graham had been and allowed him to sit beside her, introducing herself as Jan and asking him if she could get a ride in the sailboat later. Eyewitnesses saw her begin to gather her bag and pull her clothes on, standing with Bundy and walking off the beach in the direction of the parking lot. One of them, a female housewife, found Ted's behavior with the sling slightly off, believing it was all an act.

Bundy had been able to convince Janice Ott to leave with him.

Four hours passed, full of rape and torture. Janice Ott would be forced to endure the abuse in a nearby, secluded location. Ted did to her whatever he wanted, and the worst part is that he did not kill her when he was done. No. Bundy wanted to bring somebody else to the party, and he wanted Ott to be fully conscious and aware when he did.

So, around four in the afternoon, Ted went in search of a fresh victim.

A sixteen-year-old girl named Sindi Siebenham recalled being approached by a stranger in a sling. During the time that passed between Bundy successfully pulling Janice Ott from the beach and his return to the same place, he had lost his previous charm and calm manner. When he asked Sindi for help, she noted how his eyes were shifty and his expression was nervous—clearly, there was something behind his request for help that put her off and made her leave as quickly as possible, despite his intense insistence. Other women claimed he was hiding in the restroom and would emerge and attempt to convince them to follow him to his car.

He failed several times.

But then he had success. At just before five that afternoon, one of his attempts at capturing his second and last victim of the day worked. Poor Denise Naslund had no idea.

Denise, a nineteen-year-old computer programming student, went to the beach with her boyfriend, her dog, and two friends. After enjoying a picnic with a few beers and a joint to spice things up, Denise had a fight with her boyfriend. They argued over something meaningless, and Denise headed off to the restroom to calm down. Nobody stopped her, and this fact would probably haunt them forever.

A man with a sling had been walking back and forth under the shadow of the building where the restrooms were located, but nobody had become suspicious of him. Once Denise had finished in the bathroom, an eyewitness saw her talking to the man, who seemingly approached her randomly. It was the last time she was ever seen alive.

When she did not return, Denise's boyfriend, friends, and family immediately knew that something had happened. Unfortunately, their intuitions were correct. Miss Naslund was tortured and raped, likely forced to watch as Janice Ott was killed before she herself was also murdered by Bundy. He knew he had been seen by many. He had made a big mistake, but still, he dealt with the corpses accordingly—decapitating them and discarding the skulls two miles east of Lake Sammamish State Park, not very far away from where he had killed them. The bodies were lost for good, yet nobody knew this.

Law enforcement and volunteers in the area decided to help search for the two missing women, some believing they had drowned and divers went to the bottom of the lake to search for any sign of either body. Others searched nearby forests and looked far and wide for any sign of them. Local sex offenders were brought in to police stations and questioned, but nothing came of it. There was disbelief—around forty thousand people had been in or around the Lake at the time of the abductions. How could the two women simply disappear off the face of the earth? Nobody wanted to accept there had been foul play involved. What type of deranged individual would be so bold as to kidnap in broad daylight, surrounded by a crowd?

Meanwhile, Ted arrived at the home of Elizabeth Kloepfer, or Meg Anders, who he had seen that morning and interrogated her to find out where she was going—primarily to make sure she had not been planning on visiting Lake Sammamish. Meg noted that the cold he had been suffering from for the past few days was worse than ever. When she asked what was wrong with him, he explained he had spent the day cleaning his car and helping his landlord, and it had made his symptoms worse. Still, he was hungry and wanted to eat some burgers at a downtown bowling alley. Meg accepted the invite to go with him and brought her daughter along. Later, she remembered how he ate as if he was famished, wolfing down two burgers and insisting on an ice cream. His behavior was strange and it made Meg feel uncomfortable, but she never said a word.

The days passed, and nobody managed to find anything that could lead them to these two missing women. A sketch of a man who witnesses had heard introduce himself as 'Ted' was released by the police and published in the Seattle Times the following week. The sketch was accompanied by a brief description that said the suspect drove a metallic Volkswagen.

Meg was at work when one of her colleagues chuckled out loud and asked her if the man did not look a bit like *her* Ted and even drove a Volkswagen to match. Meg laughed nervously but remembered how suspicious her partner had been on the day of the disappearances and how he had attacked her on a previous occasion when they were riding a raft down a river, and he had dumped her in the water, making no move to help her get back in the raft. She had seen something in his eyes that had terrified her.

Meg's mind began to fill with a terrible thought—wondering if perhaps she had gotten involved with a dangerous killer. She watched how a month passed and no positive news of the investigation was released. A five-thousand-dollar reward was offered for information, but even the best eyewitness accounts came to nothing. One claim of the man's British accent led police to believe that perhaps the kidnapper was a Canadian serial killer on the loose.

Meg decided it was time to call the hotline, which had been created to assist with the investigation, but a friend decided to speak for her. They called from a payphone and made sure to confirm if the Volkswagen in question was metallic and not dull like Ted's, and if its owner had been wearing a wristwatch at the time. Relief spread through Meg as the person on the other side of the phone responded that all reports had spoken of a metallic paint on the vehicle. Meg and her friend hung up before asking about the watch

Other people, too, recognized Ted as the most likely individual identified in the sketch, but after police did a quick search of his records for possible criminal records, concluded that a law student without any run-ins with the police could not be connected to the disappearances.

The weeks continued to pass, and Meg no longer felt as suspicious about her quiet, enigmatic boyfriend as she had been previously. She traveled to Salt Lake City to pick up her daughter and began to look for an apartment for Ted, who was going to transfer from his law school to the one at the University of Utah, after receiving an acceptance at the beginning of the month.

When she met Ted at the terminal, she was shocked to see he had cut his hair short and looked like a completely different person. In his mind, he knew there was a noose closing on him in Seattle, and he had to move away from all that heat.

He left Seattle for Utah on September 2nd. Not long after, people started realizing that the disappearances in the former city had stopped, and without linking it to Ted Bundy's departure from the city, they finally felt they could relax.

This was not the case, however. Five days later, two men were hunting on an old logging road a few miles away from Lake Sammamish, when one of them stepped on a human skeleton. He ran back to his jeep to bring the other man with him, and together with two teenagers who had been walking through the area, returned to find not only a skeleton but a hairless skull. Searching further, they found a clump of black hair, which belonged to Denise Naslund, and some strands of blonde hair, Janice Ott's, and a third skeleton missing its head, Georgeann Hawkins.

Six months later, forestry students would discover the skulls and mandibles of Lynda Ann Healy, Susan Rancourt, Roberta Kathleen Parks, and Brenda Ball on Taylor Mountain—another of the killer's personal graveyards.

These discoveries would chill the bones of local citizens for decades. The deathly mark that Ted Bundy left on Seattle would not disappear for many years, and even now, he is still remembered.

Now with Ted in Utah, it was the beginning of a new chapter of death and defilement.

VI

A New Chapter

TED BUNDY MAY HAVE BEEN SPENDING HIS TIME with Meg Anders, but he was by no means faithful to her—he was known to have been going out with at least a dozen other women. He began a completely new life in Utah, studying the law curriculum for the second time and preparing himself for another killing spree.

Something bothered him as he began his classes at this fresh house of studies; the level of difficulty had increased greatly and he found himself lost. It was a great disappointment to him. It was like a wall was crashing when he realized he could not start over and obtain a law degree with ease.

Bundy did not take long to begin his murders once more in this new city. In fact, it is believed that only nineteen days after killing the two women near Lake Sammamish and setting out toward Utah, he may have stopped in Vancouver, Washington, and murdered twenty-year-old hitchhiker Carol Valenzuela. Her corpse was found in a shallow grave along with another young victim named Martha Morrison, seventeen-years-old, both with signs of strangulation.

Police have never confirmed these murders, but the two suspects are Ted Bundy, and another killer named Warren Leslie Forrest.

Bundy also killed a hitchhiker in Idaho, raped and strangled. She is, to this day, still unidentified, and Bundy himself has offered mixed confessions about what he did to her corpse. He told one biographer he had disposed of the remains in a nearby river after doing his deeds, while he told Ann Rule that he returned the next day to photograph the woman's corpse and dismember it.

He then moved on to kidnap sixteen-year-old Nancy Wilcox, a cheerleader, on October 2nd in a suburb of Salt Lake City and dragged her into a wooded area where he raped her. Although he initially intended to release her—or so he would claim—she would not stop screaming, he was forced to strangle her. He buried her remains near Capitol Reef National Park. Neither were ever found.

On October 18th, Ted targeted Melissa Smith, the seventeen-year-old daughter of a local police chief. She had been heading to a slumber party when it had been canceled but decided not to waste a perfectly good Friday night and went instead to a pizza parlor with a friend. Upon leaving the place, she decided to hitchhike back home. There are mixed eyewitness reports of what happened next—some claim she got into a car and was taken away, others claim they saw her pass by their home before letting out a scream.

But the truth is that Bundy assaulted her with a crowbar, whacking her in the head so hard he knocked her unconscious. The blow fractured her skull and may have put her asleep for days—it is believed she was held for five days in Ted's apartment, while he satisfied his sexual urges with her.

Eventually, he grew tired of Melissa and wrapped one of his socks around her throat, pulling it tight until she died. Her body was found on a brush-covered hillside in Summit County, Utah. She was nude, and Bundy's navy-blue sock was still wrapped around her neck. She had been bathed, hair cleaned, nails painted, and makeup applied to her face. The dead girl had been cared for despite her abduction. This horrified investigators and everyone who found out later. Furthermore, the fact the killer had attacked the daughter of Chief Louis Smith made the public feel that nobody was safe and the boogeyman they had heard of in Washington State was now in Utah. Fear filled the community. No young woman was allowed to leave their home at night.

Still, there are always rebels. Even the strictest or more careful parents can always find themselves tricked or defeated by their children, who, in their innocence, know how to manipulate Mom and Dad to get what they want. It is exactly how the next girl became Bundy's victim.

The problem is, Bundy felt free once more. Free to hurt so many, as he had in Washington without the worry of an investigation breathing down his neck. He knew he was not a monstrosity, who stood out to the general public; his criminal record was squeaky clean. He was charming, handsome, successful, and women generally trusted his intentions. It was like being invisible to society, even when he was one of its greatest menaces.

Laura Ann Aime, seventeen-years-old, was one such girl who did not pay attention to the warnings of her parents. She was a free-spirited girl almost six-feet-tall, weighing one hundred forty pounds; if riding horses did not scare her, no rumors of a nighttime murderer would either. Laura's parents had taken the news seriously and told her not to hitchhike at night—this was the way the infamous killer was getting his victims. Laura, brave, and surrounded by the naive teenage foolishness of invincibility, told her mother she would take care of herself.

Laura was living with a friend, south of Salt Lake City. Since quitting school, she had been hanging out with undesirable company, and her parents were trying hard to put her back on the road to success and a good life. They called and visited her occasionally, trying to accomplish the change they so desired. Unfortunately, tragedy was about to strike their lives.

On October 31st, Laura left home and headed to a party in the suburbs of Orem, just ten miles north of her home. She enjoyed herself there but left just after midnight to return home. She was in the city of Lehi and would need to hitchhike down Highway 89 to return home. She started out with no fear anything could happen to her. What were the odds of coming across a serial killer on this cold night, so far away from his hunting ground?

Yet Bundy *was* there in the area, hunting for a girl just like Laura.

Since Laura and her parents only talked occasionally, when their first call went answered, they did not react. However, when a planned hunting trip with her father came and went and Laura did not show up, they knew something was wrong.

Indeed it was. Laura had been kept at Bundy's apartment; beaten, raped, and sodomized before he strangled her to death with a sock, just like Melissa Smith. Her body was found in American Fork Canyon on Thanksgiving Day of the same year.

Ted's next attack, however, would be different. It would signal Ted Bundy's first major mistake and the beginning of his downfall. Of this attack, much is known and little is speculation. Why? Surprisingly, Bundy's victim managed to escape alive. Undeniably, it was the very attack that would symbolize Ted's eventual demise, even though he would kill after.

Enter Carol DaRonch.

At around five in the afternoon, having been at a dentist appointment in the morning, eighteen-year-old Carol DaRonch left her home and set off in the direction of Fashion Place Mall to purchase a gift. As she passed the department store Sears, she was approached by a good-looking man with a neatly trimmed mustache and long hair. He identified himself as Officer Roseland

and asked her if she had a car in the parking lot. She answered she did, and he replied a suspect had been seen breaking into her car. He urged her to come with him to see if it had been damaged or to check if anything was missing. 'Officer Roseland' walked with long strides, and they arrived at the car within moments.

When they reached her Camaro, it was undamaged and seemed to be in the same state she had left it in. This seemed strange to Carol; however, she obeyed the officer's instruction to open the driver's door. When he instructed her to also open the passenger door, she refused, finding it unnecessary. He then asked her to follow him to locate his partner, who he claimed was holding the suspect. By now, it was around seven in the evening.

As the minutes passed with DaRonch accompanying him in his search, Bundy told her his partner and their suspect were probably at a police substation across from the mall; it was a building that actually served as a laundromat. She felt confused and suspicious but could not identify a definite sign that confirmed her suspicions—the officer was well-dressed, spoke well, and behaved professionally, just as any police officer would. After reaching the cleaners, he found the building's side door locked and told her to follow him around to his vehicle so they could go to the police station.

When she asked him for identification, the false officer laughed, flashed a badge, and put it away before getting into his Volkswagen. He locked the doors and drove, heading to a residential area.

Before Carol could ask him what was going on, Ted pulled the car over violently and attacked her, throwing a handcuff on to her right wrist. They struggled and she scratched his face, but he brandished the handcuff once more and placed it on...*the same wrist*. He was unaware that this action would save her. Carol threw her hand up to catch Bundy's wrist as he swung it toward her; a crowbar in his grip would have cracked open her skull, but she pushed it away. At that moment, she saw the perfect chance to escape; jumping out of the car and running down the street, disappearing in the darkness.

Bundy pounced out of the vehicle and considered following her for a moment, but it would almost certainly expose him to the neighbors in the nearby homes, so he got back in his car and sped away. He drove, feeling confused and angry, and, most importantly, defeated. Defeat did not make Ted Bundy weaker—it only gave him a stronger desire to succeed and satisfy his never-ending hunger and unquenchable thirst for blood, pain, and tears.

Where another killer may have returned home to lick his wounds, or at least take a night off to reflect on what had gone wrong, Theodore Bundy considered it a good idea to find a fresh victim; someone he could hurt like he had wanted to hurt Carol DaRonch. He drove nineteen miles north of Murray toward the city of Bountiful. A high school, Viewmont High, was hosting a musical, where he could easily find a victim fitting the typical characteristics he desired.

His victim was there. Seventeen-year-old student, Debra Jean Kent, was about to become Ted Bundy's latest toy.

Witnesses would recall seeing a stranger standing behind the auditorium, behaving strangely, and trying to conceal himself. He had also asked a teacher and a student to accompany him to the parking lot to identify a car, but neither of them agreed to follow him. However, it is believed at one point, he managed to lure the young Debra in the same manner and took her away. Not much is known of Debra's death or what Bundy did with her body—she was considered a missing person until only an hour before Bundy's execution. A single kneecap belonging to Debra was the only part found in the area where investigators and family members searched. Her family was torn apart by her death, as well as the grief of her brother dying at twenty-six in a car accident.

Elizabeth Kloepfer—Meg Anders—was alarmed when she read that young women were now disappearing in the Salt Lake City area; all but confirming Bundy was the man behind it. Without a moment's hesitation, she called the county police once more in November and was invited to the station for an interview by a detective.

By now, Ted was considered as one of the suspects in the disappearances, but witnesses had not been able to identify him in photos, probably due to his new look. Nothing came out of this interview with Meg. She called again a month later; a call which helped put Bundy's name on the list of prime suspects. Still, not enough evidence linked him to the murders other than descriptions of his car, and Bundy continued his activities.

Continued reports of murders and the current ongoing investigation near Salt Lake City, caused Bundy to push his murders elsewhere by 1975. On January 12th, he took his first Colorado victim. Her name was Caryn Eileen Campbell, a twenty-three-year-old short-haired nurse staying at a lodge called *Wildwood Inn*. As she walked down a hallway to her room after stepping out of the elevator, Bundy knocked her out cold with a crowbar and abducted her.

Despite the well-lit hallway and Bundy having to descend to the ground floor with a body, on his way to his car, he pulled it off, and was able to have his way with Caryn at a more private location. Her nude body was found buried in snow just outside the resort a month later. She had been cut with a sharp instrument and her head had been bludgeoned.

About a hundred miles northeast of this inn, a twenty-six-year-old ski instructor, who went by the name of Julie Cunningham, went missing as she walked to a date with her friend. Bundy's confession stated he approached the woman on crutches and asked her for help to get some gear into his car. He whacked Julie on the head with a club and handcuffed her, taking her to a remote location where he raped and strangled her. Bundy returned to Julie's remains six weeks later for unknown reasons; it is believed he saw his victims' corpses as trophies.

Bundy struck again on April 6th, 1975. His victim this time was Denise Lynn Oliverson, who had just had an argument with her husband and hopped on her bike to ride to her parents' home and cool down. She never made it. At some point along Route 50, she was intercepted by Bundy, who abducted and killed her. This murder was another credited to him only after his confession prior to execution, and Oliverson's body has never been located.

Ted cared little for the ages of the women he attacked, as long as they were pretty and could guarantee him sexual release. His next victim was only twelve; a junior high school student named Lynette Dawn Culver, who boarded a bus bound for Fort Hall. She was never seen again. Bundy would go on to claim he had abducted her and taken her to a room at the *Holiday Inn*, drowned her in the bathtub, and sexually assaulted her before disposing of the body in a river. Whether this is true or not, Lynette's body has never been found.

In May, Bundy became occupied with the visit of three co-workers, including Carole Anne Boone, who would go on to establish a serious relationship with him, as well as a one-week trip with Meg Anders to Seattle, where they discussed marriage. Meg did not mention the three times she had called the police or the interview she'd had with a detective, and Bundy kept his on-and-off relationship with Boone and a Utah law student secret, as well. It was a failing relationship that could barely be called a connection at all, but it would not last much longer.

June followed, and with it came fresh blood: Susan Curtis, a hazel-eyed fifteen-year-old who had traveled by bicycle to a youth conference at Brigham Young University in Provo, Utah. She attended a formal banquet with her friends and fellow students, before heading back to her dormitory to brush her teeth, as she wore braces. She was never seen again. She joined Nancy Wilcox, Debra Kent, Julie Cunningham, Lynette Culver, and Denise Oliverson in the list of bodies never recovered, despite Bundy offering the general location of their buried remains.

Two months later, Bundy claimed to have found God and became a member of the Church of Jesus Christ of Latter-day Saints. It is believed that he joined this faith due to the possibility of finding new, unsuspecting victims he could lure with false pretenses more than actually adopting religious beliefs. After his conviction, he received ex-communication by the church. When asked what religious affiliation he had, Bundy stated he was a Methodist.

Whatever was going through Ted's mind, there was pressure starting to build around him. Investigators, who were analyzing the murder spree in and around Washington State, had developed a database which allowed them to narrow down the names of people related to the victims in some way; classmates, acquaintances, owners named Ted, who had Volkswagens, sex offenders—as well as other important characteristics—and when they finally were able to get results from their archaic computer, only twenty-six names appeared on four of those lists.

Ted Bundy was one of those names. Meanwhile, the detectives, still stuck in a time when computers were not as reliable as they are in modern times, compiled a manual list that included similar characteristics that could narrow down the one hundred best suspects for the spree...

...Bundy was on that list, as well.

The problem was not just that Ted was part of those lists for the Northwest killing spree, either. It was the fact that he had moved to Utah, where similar crimes were now taking place.

Ted Bundy was now suspect number one on every list, and he would have to tread lightly.

He would try, of course, but as the old adage goes, *every swine will get his comeuppance.* Ted Bundy's life was about to become miserable.

VII

Unmasked

BUNDY WAS NEVER AN OVERLY-CONFIDENT killer in the way others are. Sure, he may have attacked in broad daylight on occasion or continued abducting and murdering women despite knowing there were strong investigations aimed at him, but he always did well to mask his true self and kept from revealing the demon within his heart—until he was safely behind a door.

Bundy managed to convince his political allies, peers, and professors that he was a normal—even bright and hard-working—human being, and women were charmed by him; after all, not all women he slept with were his victims. His mask was the most powerful thing he had; it managed to keep the police away. Experienced detectives were having strong doubts this law student, without any adult criminal history, was capable of hurting so many innocent females.

But the mask would fall off, naturally, as Bundy slipped up. Because every killer—or at least, *almost any killer*—slips up sooner or later. Luckily, in this case, it was due more to an observant police officer doing his job than Bundy actually making a mistake.

On the night of August 16th, 1975, Ted Bundy drove to the neighborhood of Granger, a Salt Lake City suburb and the second-largest city of Utah, in the hopes of finding a young woman to terrorize. He cruised around the area until the early hours of the morning, hoping to find a new victim. But someone else was also in the area—somebody who would end the killer's spree—at least for the time being.

An officer in a patrol car had been watching Bundy in his car, driving around suspiciously. Igniting his engine, he began following Ted. He recalled how Bundy sped up and fled the area as soon as he became aware of his pursuer, but it was too late.

The officer stopped Bundy and ordered him to open his passenger door. There he found a ski mask, another mask made from pantyhose, a crowbar, handcuffs, trash bags, a rope, an ice pick, a flashlight, and other suspicious objects. The officer immediately concluded that Bundy was a burglar, although the killer had explanations for why he was carrying each item.

Unfortunately for Ted, however, the officer had been following the case of the disappearing women and recalled how Carol DaRonch had described a similar vehicle belonging to the man who attacked her. He had also been informed that Elizabeth Kloepfer had reported her fears about Ted Bundy, owner of a tan Volkswagen, during a 1974 phone call, and these facts rang all of his alarm bells.

He arrested Bundy and a search of his apartment took place shortly thereafter; police found a guide to Colorado ski resorts belonging to the Wildwood Inn and a brochure advertising the play at the school where Bundy had kidnapped Debra Kent. Ironically enough, they did not search well enough to find the Polaroids of his victims.

Bundy was released due to a lack of evidence but was immediately placed under twenty-four-hour surveillance. Now it was just a matter of finding something that would stick and put him behind bars. Meg Anders was called, with detectives requesting an interview with her. Only now did the officers take heed of poor Meg's words.

Meg told the detectives how Ted had possessed many stolen objects and was always in debt. She also spoke of how he sometimes took her vehicle—also a Volkswagen Beetle—out at night instead of his, and he had not been with her on the nights the detectives found he had killed the Pacific Northwest victims, as well as the fateful Sunday when he had murdered Janice Ott and Denise Naslund.

All of the pieces began to fall in to place, and it was clear that Ted Bundy had been the murderer all along. Detectives moved to locate Ted's vehicle, but he had sold it to somebody just weeks before. It was located, impounded, and FBI technicians searched it, finding hairs identical to those of three victims.

To make matters worse for the increasingly desperate killer, Carol DaRonch was called in to view him in a lineup; amidst desperate sobs, she immediately identified him as the dreaded 'Officer Roseland,' who had attacked her so viciously after fooling her into trusting him. He was also picked out by witnesses around the auditorium at Viewmont High School, condemning him. As of yet, there was not enough evidence to link him with any murders, but Carol DaRonch's kidnapping and assault landed him criminal charges the police had wanted to pin on him since his arrest. He was bailed out by his parents for the sum of fifteen thousand dollars, but things had just begun to get ugly for Bundy.

Bundy was not just seen as the man who had attacked an innocent woman and possibly kidnapped and murdered another; he was strongly believed to be the culprit of over a dozen abductions and/or murders, and police were working their hardest to find any evidence that would help charge him with as many of them as possible. He moved in permanently with Elizabeth in Seattle— unaware that she was the reason the police were so sure he was the killer, and spent most of his time awaiting his indictment and trial. Surveillance became so intrusive that Kloepfer claimed that whenever she and Ted stepped out of the home to go out somewhere, so many cars started up that "It sounded like the beginning of the Indy 500."

A great meeting took place in November, where three investigators, one for each state where Bundy had murdered, met in Colorado and re-collected information with dozens of detectives and prosecutors from five states. The conclusion of the meeting left them with no doubt; Ted Bundy was the killer they were looking for and was just a matter of finding enough evidence to charge him with the murders.

His trial began February 23rd, 1976, Bundy accepting his attorney's advice of waiving his right to a jury; they both considered it would work against him, thanks to the media version of the crimes he was being accused of. Bundy was found guilty of kidnapping and assault a week later. Judge Stewart Hanson Jr. sentenced him to a minimum of one and a maximum of fifteen years in the Utah State Prison.

While imprisoned, Bundy was subject to a psychiatric evaluation. Doctors concluded that Bundy was neither psychotic nor suffered from substance addiction. He had no mental illness or lesions; in truth, he was of enviable mental health. An initial diagnosis of bipolar disorder was soon discarded, and experts concluded he was most likely an individual possessing a subtype of antisocial personality disorder (ASPD); basically and in layman's terms, Ted Bundy was a *sociopath* or *psychopath*. He was an expert manipulator that seemed to 'shift' from one persona to another, with one of Bundy's own aunts describing later how she had watched him turn in to a stranger on a dark night as they had stood waiting for a train. He had a lack of guilt or remorse that was characteristic of those diagnosed with similar disorders and evidence of narcissism and poor judgment that came with them.

But even while Ted was closely watched at the prison, and his mind was being studied like a test subject, Bundy was already planning his escape. In fact, it would only be four months after his initial incarceration before he actually made his first move.

In October, he was found hiding in some bushes with a kit that included road maps, airline schedules, and a social security card. He was apprehended and sent to solitary confinement for several weeks. Not long after, he was charged with the murder of Caryn Campbell, the nurse he had taken from the *Wildwood Inn* hallway. In January 1977, Bundy was transferred to Aspen.

After only a few months, what followed was an extreme mix of ineptitude and Bundy's own luck—the same luck that had gotten him this far. The killer was about to pull off something that would only be read in thriller stories or watched in movies—Theodore Bundy was about to escape in a most epic fashion.

His new trial, for the murder of Caryn Campbell, was a peculiar one. Ted lost faith in his legal team, viewing them as both inefficient and inept at their duties, or perhaps with an escape plan already forming in his head, Ted decided to serve as his own attorney—a legal right allowed to all citizens but further reinforced in this particular case because Ted Bundy was a law student.

Consequently, Ted was allowed to remain within the courtroom without handcuffs or leg shackles that would have been worn in any other trial situation, an obvious oversight which proved Bundy's natural ability to charm or generate trust within those he encountered. After all, nobody believed he was going to attempt to get away from the courtroom, much less escape the entire city and disappear into the mountains…

…but he did. Oh, yes…this heinous killer with no regard for another human life, knew what he had done. Bundy was not prepared to be locked in a cell, as more of his hidden graveyards were discovered. He could foresee his sentence slowly turning in to one of death. Bundy knew he needed to get away and soon, if he wished to remain free.

The question was just a matter of *when*? Well, *when* had finally come. On June 7th, 1977, when he was transported from Garfield County jail to Pitkin County Courthouse in Aspen.

Ted began the trial listening to opening statements, but due to the amount of paperwork he was going to face, he took advantage of a recess to ask for a chance to visit the courthouse's law library so he could research similar cases and attain any information that could aid in his defense. The request was granted, and Ted was allowed to enter the library with little surveillance.

He walked away from the entrance and began to move from bookshelf to bookshelf, appearing to look for something specific, but was trying to get both as far away from the guard escorting him and as close to one of the windows as possible.

At one point, having grown tired of the act, he disappeared behind a shelf and opened a window. Peering out, he could see the drop from the second floor he was on—it was no joke—to fall all that way down to the ground was risky, but in truth, he had no choice. *It was now or never.* Thus, setting in motion the decision he had all along—to escape.

A woman recalled seeing a man throw himself out the window and landing on the ground uncomfortably. Curiously, she asked a nearby police officer if this was normal behavior at the courthouse. In spite of the officer immediately sprinting in the direction she had seen Ted, the officer arrived too late. Ted had landed his jump badly, spraining his right ankle as he hit the ground, but adrenaline and desperation kept him upright and pushed him on, pulling off his outer layer of clothes to keep eyewitnesses guessing.

Law enforcement soon began to share the terrible news from one officer to the next: *Ted Bundy had escaped*. Roadblocks were set up all around town. Bundy crossed the city without a choice, having no vehicle to escape in, but went undetected and managed to disappear into the Aspen Mountains. He was wearing a t-shirt and shorts, making him look like just another tourist. Now outside the city limits, he had managed to free himself of the constant worry that the roadblocks brought him, but he had a new issue; he needed to find food, water, and shelter.

Now that he was already a fugitive, he did not have to worry about charm or his public image: all he needed was to take what he required and survive. On the mountain, he found a cabin. He broke into it and found food, clothing, and a rifle.

Bundy stayed at the cabin that night. When morning came, Bundy continued south toward a town named Crested Butte, but lost his way and began to wander aimlessly around the mountain. Two days of sleeplessness and pain followed. His sprained ankle was getting worse in the harsh cold, and Bundy knew he was in danger of being caught at any time.

With each passing day, Bundy was feeling increasingly weak. He decided to risk everything and go back to Aspen, where he could find a car and escape the area entirely. It was not the best plan, but it was the only one he had. This idea took him past the roadblocks and led him to narrowly miss search parties along the way. He found a car with the keys still in the ignition. Such luck was not only incredible but also extremely unlikely—it was as if Bundy had been blessed, somehow, though at the time, he did not feel that way.

Luck would not be enough. Two police officers spotted a car weaving from side to side as it drove along the streets of the city. They pulled the car over and finally came across the man they had been searching for over the past six days. He did not resist arrest. It was not long before he was back in Garfield County jail.

One escape had been incredible and unlikely enough. How would he be able to pull off another, especially with law enforcement making sure he never got the chance to make them look like fools again?

As the old saying goes, "never say never."

VIII

Unstoppable

ESCAPING PRISON WAS NOT JUST A DESIRE THAT any man stuck in a cage might feel; it was a need that drove Bundy crazy.

He knew how much he needed the outside world and what it brought him: women to unleash his fantasies upon, people to charm and earn the trust, and of course, the means to calm his massive ego, and a drive that had kept him going this far.

Theodore Bundy was not a man to be locked up in a cell.

Even so, many among his inner circle—as well as experts who studied the case—believed he was foolish and impatient for thinking of escape. His trial was falling to pieces. Most of the evidence found, the prosecutors had hoped to use against him, was inadmissible. It looked like Bundy was only going to serve the conviction on the DaRonch case—of which there were less than two years left. He had a strong chance of being a free man as soon as his conviction ended, and possibly avoid facing future trials because of his latest victory.

Bundy was obsessed with getting out, no matter what the cost. The fact his new partner and former co-worker, Carole Ann Boone, was smuggling cash into the prison for him and helping him plan his next escape did not help to deter him either. Carole wished to be near him, despite knowing what he had done—this would not change, even after it was clear he had killed dozens of women in the most heinous way. She would change her entire life for the man she loved so dearly. Other fans, men and women who deeply admired the killer, also pitched in with their own cash and respect, further fueling his deluded belief he was not doing anything wrong at all— that he was right.

Along with the cash he received from Boone, Bundy was also able to acquire a detailed floor plan of the jail, along with a hacksaw.

Allow me to break the fourth wall for a moment, reader, and inform you that what you are about to read is something you would have never imagined somebody doing outside of a movie. Ted Bundy was able to hide the hacksaw for weeks. Every night he took advantage of the noise his fellow prisoners made while showering, to saw a discreet square-shaped hole in the light fixture above his bed without detection. Something else to point out—there were steel bars in the ceiling, and yet he found a way to saw between them without anybody noticing.

Now it was just a case of being patient because Bundy had a problem to solve; he did not fit through the hole. Nobody seemed to wonder why Ted was losing so much weight. This diabolical killer was steadily eating less to shed the pounds to become thin enough to fit through the one-foot-by-one-foot square in his ceiling. The day did come, though, when he finally found himself thirty-five pounds thinner and able to pull himself up into the crawl space beyond the hole. Nobody saw him enter the space. One prisoner complained of movement in the ceiling of his cell, but his claim was ignored.

It was late 1977, and pre-trial motions had become tedious and seemingly endless. The prosecutor wished to link Bundy with missing girls in Utah, and the Aspen trial started to receive increased attention nationally. Bundy wanted the trial moved, preferably to Denver, perhaps already having a plan around this new change. The trial judge granted one half of that request: the trial would be moved, but not to Denver. Colorado Springs was chosen, and it was noted how the judge had chosen a place where the juries were traditionally hostile toward suspected killers.

None of that would matter anyway, as Bundy had only been biding time for his grand escape just a few weeks later on December 30th.

The night was dark and quiet, with jail authorities allowing their staff to return home with their families for Christmas time, and many of the non-violent prisoners had been granted a brief leave—an attempt to alleviate the stress on the jail's budget. Bundy had practiced his escape enough by then and knew exactly where he would go after leaving his crawl space. It was risky—in fact, it was one of the riskiest places to go in the entire prison—Ted planned to emerge from the crawl space into the chief jailer's apartment.

And as incredibly insane as it may sound, the escape was a complete success.

At seven in the morning on December 31st, 1977, a prison guard walked past Bundy's cell and left him breakfast, thinking the prisoner lying in bed was still sleeping. The guard continued his task, moving away without a second thought. It was not until a few hours later when guards began to notice that Bundy had not been seen during the day that they ran to his cell and found the food tray still there, untouched, and decided to open his cell door.

What a surprise it must have been for them, when they pulled his blanket back and found only pillows and books underneath, and no sign of their prisoner—just the square-shaped edges of the hole he had cut in the ceiling above him. Bundy had simulated the shape of his sleeping body and climbed up into the crawlspace before wriggling his way to the section of the ceiling above the chief jailer's apartment. The owner of the room had been out that night celebrating with his wife—something Ted had probably already known, most likely from a source within the prison—Ted had undressed, put the jailer's clothes on, to literally walk out the front door of the prison without being challenged at all.

Bundy had then stolen a car and driven east before it broke down, and he was forced to request a ride from a passing driver. The person took him sixty miles east. It would be one of the rare people who had been in the same car as Bundy and survived to tell the tale. Ted soon found himself on a bus heading to Denver. There, he traveled to the airport and took a flight to Chicago. It was at this point, over fifteen hours later, that the aforementioned discovery of his escape was even noticed by the guards.

Laughable, or as silly as it all happened, the killer was on the loose once more, and he had decided to change his ways after being imprisoned. In fact, he was as bad as he had been before, if not worse, but he now had the added distinction of evading law enforcement. Gone was the impulsive desire that had gotten him so close to spending his life in prison; now, he wanted to turn over a new leaf. Ted was going to do things right, this time around.

Or actually, he was going to do wrong things much more efficiently than he had before.

Ted Bundy was going on one last spree that would cement his status as one of the—if not the most—fearsome serial killers in U.S. history.

IX

One Last Time

TED NEVER BELIEVED HE WAS GOING TO BE stopped.

He believed he was now probably the most wanted man in the entire nation. Not only had he committed terrible, heinous crimes across several states, but he had also escaped jail twice and put law enforcement on maximum alert. He had followed the investigation for years now and knew he could not allow himself to be captured. The public was still divided in its opinion; some said he was being framed for political reasons, but he was fully aware that the people who mattered could put him away, or worse.

Once he had arrived in Chicago, the killer knew he had to keep moving. There were more distant places he could go that would put a larger distance between him and Colorado and the law enforcement along the way. He knew that traveling to the furthest extreme of the country was the most plausible idea at the time.

Bundy later confessed that he had briefly wanted to truly retire from his criminal activity if it meant staying out of prison. He resolved to begin working somewhere legitimate that could represent an entirely new start to his life. However, as soon as Ted was asked for identification on his first and only job application, he decided he did not really have a chance at finding a proper job or starting over. Ted Bundy returned to his old wanderings. Whether this is the truth from the killer's own lips, or simply one of Bundy's attempts to humanize his image and charm the court, as his final trials took place, we may never know.

His spree would end similarly to how it had begun in Washington—with the murder of young college students on a university campus.

Having escaped Garfield County jail in spectacular fashion and managing to advance toward Chicago without anybody on his tail, Ted began to cross states as he headed toward Florida. His first move was to travel to Michigan, by train, on the first days of January in 1978, where he stayed for around five days and lay low to avoid being recognized by eyewitnesses.

By now, he was on the FBI's Most Wanted list and had appeared in national news reports and papers, so it was no longer a game of local cat and mouse, which he had excelled at for years—it was more a case of being the sole objective of thousands of highly-focused police efforts—police under constant pressure to achieve results.

Once his time in Michigan had reached an end, the killer stole a car and drove to Atlanta. Then he ditched the ride and took a bus to Tallahassee, Florida, on January 8th. He was going under a new identity, Chris Hagen, and rented a room at a house near the campus of Florida State University.

It was around this time that his aforementioned job interview took place, but he quickly returned to looking for easier, less legitimate ways of finding money—he regularly shoplifted and pickpocketed women's credit cards to keep him going.

During this time, Bundy was already planning his next lethal attack on innocent women in the most obvious location, although nobody would have imagined that it would take place so soon after he had narrowly escaped justice.

The thing is, Florida State University possessed a sorority house that Bundy had been keeping an eye on since he had arrived at the boarding house he was living in. Chi Omega was home to a group of around forty young, beautiful women, who Ted watched hungrily, and waited for the perfect moment.

On the cold, dark night of January 15th, 1978, with a chilling temperature of twenty degrees Fahrenheit, Bundy crept up to the sorority house and slipped inside through a back door with a damaged lock, climbing the stairs with an oak firewood club he had picked up on the campus.

It was a few minutes before three in the morning, and twenty-one-year-old Margaret Bowman slept in her bed without a care in the world, after her friend Melanie Nelson had left the room only ten minutes before. She was unaware that Ted Bundy was standing above her with his hands wrapped around the log that would end her life.

The tall, slender woman did not even get to struggle as the object descended on her head repeatedly and broke her skull open, revealing her brain. Before she could even react, Ted pulled pantyhose around her neck and tugged as hard as he could, to the point where her neck became half its normal size and broke.

The saddest part of it all? *Nobody heard a thing.*

The rest of the women were still unaware as Bundy moved quietly to the next room. One of the girls found it somewhat strange that she had seen the hallway light switch off a few minutes earlier, but she did not know why it had happened. The killer stealthily entered the room of twenty-year-old Lisa Levy, admired her body for a moment before pouncing on her and beating her senseless with the club. The girl fell unconscious and Bundy began to ravage her; sticking a hair mist bottle in her rectum and then her vagina and pulling at her nipples so fiercely with his teeth that he practically tore one off.

In his arousal, he also bit down hard on her left buttock, leaving a mark that would be crucial in identifying him. When he finally concluded his assault, he strangled her mercilessly and left the room, believing she was dead. Lisa would die on the way to the hospital, suffering horrific agony in her last moments of life.

Kathy Kleiner, twenty-one, slept next door and was next to be brutally attacked. Kathy's jaw was broken, a pain that followed her for years, and her shoulder torn open. Karen Chandler, also twenty-one, was assaulted almost simultaneously. The oak log broke her jaw with such force that several teeth burst out of her mouth. Her left arm was shattered as she attempted to defend herself. Bundy ran from the sorority house once the women started making noise.

Only fifteen minutes had passed—fifteen minutes for Bundy to destroy the lives of four women and their families. Slowly, the unharmed girls began to wake up and leave their rooms to see what was going on. One particular girl entering the house after a date would recall seeing a man holding a club in his hand as he disappeared through the front door. She and another female student ran to where Karen was stumbling along the hallway and caught sight of Kathy crying hysterically, her hands coated in blood.

Lisa Levy was slowly regaining consciousness as she lay face down on her bed and blood pooled from her cracked skull. One of the girls, still confused as to what was going on, saw the girl's wounded nipple and believed there had been a shooting inside the sorority.

It was chaos, and the peaceful, fun lives of every girl in the house were shattered for months, years in the case of the worst victims. Even with this flurry of attacks, Ted Bundy was not over for that night. He wanted more, and he would not go very far to get it.

A few blocks away in an apartment building, twenty-one-year-old Cheryl Thomas, another Florida State University student, lived alone in a basement apartment. She was sleeping and never realized Bundy had broken into her apartment. He entered her room, bludgeoned her wildly with his club, fracturing her jaw and skull in several places, as well as dislocating her shoulder. Cheryl was left permanently deaf from the attack and dancing career ruined for good. He sexually assaulted her, leaving some of his semen on the bed, as well as two hairs stuck to the pantyhose used to strangle her.

Bundy escaped into the darkness, only then fully satisfied with the acts he had committed that night. The police arrived too late to catch him, but they found the evidence left behind, representing great progress in catching the killer.

Ted was unfazed by the media reaction to his attacks. He had spoken of being a changed man on his arrival to Florida, but he had not changed at all. He was still the same monster that had left Colorado. He proved this with his next and final attack.

A manhunt ensued, but Ted Bundy eluded police. On February 8th, less than a month after attacking the women on the

Florida State University campus, Ted stole a van belonging to the university and drove east to Jacksonville, where he cruised in search of a victim. He spotted fourteen-year-old Leslie Parmenter, daughter of the city's Chief of Detectives, standing in a parking lot and he approached her, identifying himself as a firefighter.

She may have become his next victim—one may never know—but her brother, who was close by, came to see what was happening and scared Bundy away from the scene. Frustrated, the killer left Jacksonville, heading to Lake City.

His next victim would be his final one, and possibly the one that revealed to the nation, and the world, that Ted Bundy was truly an evil individual, at least in the way that we use the term.

Kimberly Dianne Leach, a twelve-year-old, straight-A junior high school student, and dearly loved by friends and family, would never have imagined what was to become of her on the fateful afternoon of February 9th, 1978. Lake City had never worried about the presence of killers, rapists, or other dangerous criminals that hunted in mostly large capital cities. Those terrible crimes seemingly so distant and foreign to the small, close-knit community.

Kimberly is believed to have been approached by Bundy, who—according to the only unreliable witness, another young girl at the school—was driving a truck around the back of the school when the girl disappeared. Though Kimberly looked a bit older to some, she was still just a child. And yet, despite her tender age and innocence, Bundy had no sense of mercy toward Kimberly. She was taken to an undisclosed location where he raped and sodomized her, finally strangling her to death like many of his other innocent female victims.

Kimberly's parents were immediately alarmed when their little girl failed to return home, as she was definitely not the type of girl to stay out after school or to run away. She was reported missing almost immediately—a two-month search following. Sadly, her body would not be found until April 7th, 1978—seven weeks later—lying in an abandoned hog pen near Suwannee River State Park; the body was too mummified due to the dry weather to be identified. Beside her was a tennis shoe she had been wearing on the day of her disappearance. The news was a bittersweet discovery for the police, community, and her family.

As for Bundy, he had left Lake City for Tallahassee and eventually stole a car. Ironically, it was a Volkswagen Beetle. He left Tallahassee altogether on February 12th. When he ran out of cash and began to suspect that police were closing in on him, he wiped everything down in the room before he left and believed it was over.

For once, though, his sixth sense had failed him; he was not necessarily running *from* a trap, he was actually running *toward* one.

After midnight on February 15th, 1978, Bundy was driving toward the Alabama state line when he was spotted by Pensacola police officer David Lee, who spotted Bundy's Orange Volkswagen and found it to be a strange sight in a place he knew so well. The officer requested a *'Wants and Warrants'* check over his radio as he put his blue lights on to pull Bundy pull over.

The tag came back with the information that would finally end Ted Bundy's rampage.

The Volkswagen was stolen.

Ted immediately accelerated, knowing that something was about to go down. The chase continued for over a mile until Bundy seemingly gave up and pulled over at an intersection. Lee was cautious about drawing his revolver as he approached the driver's side, knowing he had no back-up approaching if anything went wrong. There was no way of seeing inside the vehicle either, and the patrolman was worried there was another person in the front seat beside the driver.

Bundy saw the police officer approaching and heard the order to get out of the car. He saw the gun, and studied the officer.

In his mind, a voice told him not to go down like this. *Fight. Escape, and you will be free.*

Ted got out of the vehicle, slowly, after the officer repeated his order. He lay down on the pavement and allowed David Lee to place the handcuff on his left wrist...

...then threw himself around to kick the officer's feet from under him, then throwing a punch at the patrolman a second later. They struggled, with punches flying in both directions, David's revolver pointed awkwardly to the sky as he fired a single shot to frighten Bundy, but it was useless. Ted pushed himself off the officer and ran, sprinting south and ignoring Lee's shout to halt. David Lee caught sight of Bundy's wrist, saw the handcuff, but believed it was a gun. It was all he needed.

Bang.

Ted fell, seemingly injured. Lee ran over to him and checked the man for a wound. There was none. Bundy got up, untouched, and fought to disarm him, screaming, "Help!" repeatedly in an attempt to get somebody to save him from this situation. It did not work—Lee finally subdued the suspect and took him to his car, reading him his rights and completing the arrest successfully.

As they both rode to the jail, and Bundy faced the reality that he was truly done, the entire nation knowing exactly what he was, he repeated, "I wish you had killed me."

The most ironic part? Officer David Lee had no idea who he had just captured.

X

Justice

IT WAS A LONG DRIVE TO JAIL, AND BUNDY KNEW it was over.

Interviewed by the policeman on duty, he gave his name as Kenneth Misner, although the police immediately discovered it was not true. When he was found, Bundy had in his possession: three sets of identification, including Mr. Misner's twenty-one stolen credit cards, a stolen television, stolen tags, and a bicycle, as well as the stolen orange Volkswagen Beetle.

Bundy had resisted arrest and assaulted a police officer—which the cops still believed was to avoid being arrested for theft, and not because he was a serial killer who had raped and ended the lives of dozens of women. However, it would not be long before they *did* know the truth.

Hours passed and Bundy collapsed—weeping openly and calling everybody he could to get any legal advice. Eventually, he informed the police holding him that he was Theodore Bundy.

Not long after, he called his longtime friend Ann Rule. Ann claimed he seemed distraught and desperate as if he wanted to confess everything to her. Ann had always felt that Ted had been behind the crimes after getting to know him at work. She offered to fly over to Florida, but the police soon stopped allowing Ted to make or receive calls, and she missed her chance.

Ted Bundy confessed many of his crimes during the long night of February 16th, 1978, and the general public was informed that Ted Bundy, murderer and rapist, had committed the crimes at Chi Omega Florida State University sorority house—as well as the sprees in Colorado, Utah, Idaho, and Washington—was finally in custody, and set to stand trial within a few months.

Bundy was held in jail while the evidence was studied, to see what would be admitted at his trial and what would not; most of the evidence at Kimberly Leach's crime scene and in the car that he had been using at the time was good but not substantive in terms of incriminating him. The bite on Lisa Levy's buttock was studied by dentists, and they concluded it belonged to Bundy.

More evidence arose before his June 1979 trial, and suddenly things were looking grim for the killer. Bundy had thought of using the insanity plea, but had followed another famous case, Son of Sam, and saw it did not work as intended. Therefore, he again decided on defending himself, in spite of court-appointed attorneys.

Those within the court felt Ted was sabotaging the trial with his egocentric, irregular behavior, even angering the judge on occasion. As all of this occurred, the nation watched intently; the trial was being covered by two hundred and fifty reporters and the first to be televised nationally in the United States.

A deal began to present itself for Ted, in which he would plead guilty to killing Levy and Bowman at the sorority house, and young Kimberly Leach after abducting her. In exchange, he would be given a seventy-five-year prison sentence, which was quite positive for both sides. Bundy knew he could easily receive Florida's death penalty due to the nature of his crimes. Talks advanced, and Bundy showed signs of accepting the deal, although his true intention was to file a motion after the conviction to dismiss the plea.

Then Ted changed his mind. Suddenly, everything did not make as much sense as it had. He realized he was going to have to stand in front of the cameras and admit his guilt to the entire nation and the world; it went against everything he believed.

A man with such an ego could not show the world how flawed he was or how vicious and evil he had been. Bundy decided to refuse the deal at the last moment and continued with his strategy of manipulating the trial himself.

It did not work.

Bundy was convicted on July 24th, 1979, for the murders of both Lisa Levy and Margaret Bowman, three counts of attempted first-degree murder for his attacks on Kathy Kleiner, Karen Chandler, and Cathy Thomas, and two counts of burglary.

For these crimes, Judge Edward Cowart sentenced him to two death penalties, and Bundy's plans fell to pieces once more.

Events only got worse for him as Ted was taken to trial again a few months later for the murder of Kimberly Leach, and found guilty once again. In a desperate attempt to save himself from the worst of it, before the judge began questioning Carole Anne Boone, Ted asked her to marry him and took advantage of a Florida law that stated, if she accepted, it would now constitute a legal marriage. Therefore, she could not be required to testify against him. She accepted. Still swallowing the lies that Bundy was innocent.

Carole gave birth to a daughter a year later in October and gave her his last name. Many wondered how this *'immaculate conception'* had taken place since conjugal visits were banned at the prison. It also shed light on the fact that inmates were bribing guards to allow them time with their partners.

Eventually, Carole would give up on Ted and divorce him. Many still blame her for being instrumental in his defense, when he deserved to sink on his own, unsupported.

Ted's behavior was different in the second trial, many noting he was regularly slouched in his chair, showed more of an empty glare, and erupted in angry fits he had kept hidden so well on previous occasions. It was here that he was sentenced to death by electrocution for the third time, the one that would eventually seat him in the chair.

His famous confessions—the ones that helped books like this one get written—came after this, at the precise moment he knew he was a dead man walking. Many of them made detectives and psychologists believe he had begun killing long before his first 'known' murder in 1974, and he famously claimed to have been heavily influenced by violent pornography—stating it was the source of many killers' obsessions and fantasies.

Slowly, each confession showed just how twisted Bundy's psyche was; he believed that many of his victims had been *'asking for it'*, with the way they *'radiated vulnerability'*, and showed amazement at the fact that people had even noticed him at the scenes of his abductions.

In his mind, nobody noticed anyone else, and he took it personally that people had positively identified him on various occasions. Again and again, he demonstrated to have truly distanced himself from humanity. Psychologists spoke of how he had created enormous barriers of denial that he used to contradict reality itself.

Execution dates came and went, as appeals from the killer attempted to change his fate, albeit unsuccessfully. Sometime during his time being held at Raiford Prison, it is claimed that Ted suffered an assault by multiple prisoners, who jumped him when the guards were not watching. The attack is believed to have been a gang rape, although this was not confirmed and the killer himself denied it. Further sources stated that a death row inmate would even shower alone, so it is unlikely any rape happened at all, much less one involving several men.

Hacksaws were found in his cell in the month of July 1984, and guards realized that a steel bar in the cell's windows had been sawed through and glued back together to avoid raising suspicion. The killer was moved to a different cell after this event.

Bundy's last stay of execution occurred January 17th, 1989. He could not appeal anymore or change anybody's mind—a date for his execution was finally set.

He would die on January 24th, 1989.

This decision finally unlocked the remaining shred of humanity within Bundy, although it is possible that he simply wanted to brag about what he had done. He began to give the details of his crimes and spoke of what he had done with the bodies.

Detectives were told he had kept body parts and belongings of the victims in his apartment, and had even used Meg Anders fireplace to burn a decapitated head. He had re-enacted scenes from detective magazines with several of the victims and had killed more women than those the police knew of. Over fifty was the number

Bundy offered—over one hundred was what many in the police field truly believed.

Bundy spent the last night of his life weeping in his cell, his old confidence now gone. Forty-two witnesses watched as he was moved into the death chamber and strapped to the chair, mumbling incoherently as he prepared for the moment he had sworn would never arrive.

"Do you have any last words?" Superintendent Tom Barton asked.

"Jim and Fred," the killer managed, his voice breaking. "I'd like you to give my love to my family and friends." Jim was his lawyer. Fred was the Methodist minister present. They both nodded solemnly.

The last preparations took place, and the electrode was fastened to Bundy's head. A moment later, two thousand volts of electricity flowed through the killer's body and his form lit up, while smoke rose from his right leg. The machine was turned off and a doctor approached.

He was declared dead at seven sixteen in the morning, as people danced, set off fireworks, and chanted outside the prison, *"Burn, Bundy, burn!"*

Justice was done. The world was rid of Ted Bundy.

Conclusion

"*WHEN YOU FEEL THE LAST BIT OF BREATH leaving their body, you're looking into their eyes. A person in that situation is God!*"—Ted Bundy

The notorious killer known as Ted Bundy died with many of the details of his murders still undisclosed, taking locations of many remains, and names of victims that the police never linked to him.

Ted Bundy was the original serial killer; the one that made police change their tactics and put young American women on alert, after a time when hitchhiking and helping strangers was the norm.

Bundy was not just another mad man with a mission—Ted was a revolutionary in the art of murder and the biggest name in

American serial killer history. He was not a sick maniac with a hundred traumatic reasons to be abnormal—he was, for all intents and purposes, a man with a normal life, who had succeeded for much of his youth.

For those reasons, Ted Bundy has become such an interesting killer to study. While there is no doubt that he was a dangerous, twisted individual who deserved what he got, he is still one of the entrancing cases of crime history ever witnessed thus far.

To his victims: may you rest in peace. You did not deserve to suffer.

To Ted: may the world learn from what you did so we may become better human beings.

To fans and readers: well…

Acknowledgments

This is a special thanks to the following readers who have taken time out of their busy schedule to be part of the True Crime Seven Team. Thank you all so much for all the feedback and support!

Joan Baker, Lori Green, Joan Becker, Patricia Oliver, James Herington, Linda M Wheeler, Bonnie Kernene, Barbara Davis, Jamie Bothen, Pamela Culp

Continue Your Exploration Into

The Murderous Minds

Excerpt From Mary Flora Bell

I

Meeting Mary

MOST AMERICANS ARE FAMILIAR WITH THE legend of the Bell witch, a tale that has spawned numerous books and movies. It centers around the haunting, and alleged murder, of the patriarch of a real family named Bell, who resided in Tennessee in the 1800s.

Supposedly, the vengeful spirit of a former neighbor, the witch, creates turmoil and wreaks havoc on the family in such a terrifying manner that it affected them the rest of their lives, and two hundred years later, the story is still being told.

One hundred and fifty years after the Bell family haunting, and an ocean away, a child with the last name Bell was making headlines. Her crimes would also traumatize the families of her victims for the rest of their lives. Called a witch, devil spawn, and bad seed, Mary Flora Bell will forever be the epitome of evil to some who hear her story and to those who lost a family member to her evil deeds.

Whereas the Bell witch was supposed to have the ability to shapeshift, it would be the English government that aided Mary to shapeshift and become invisible. Mary would be granted anonymity, as would the daughter she had years later, a controversial ruling. Although victims' families understood the need to protect her daughter, it was Mary's anonymity that was at the center of the debate.

Imagine, if you will, the horrific thought that a family member had been murdered, and you are notified that the killer will soon be released, but neither you nor anyone in the public will be privy to where they will be living after their release. Now, compound that thought by adding the fact that the convicted killer will also be given a new name and identity, which authorities refuse to reveal to you. How safe would you feel? When you stepped outdoors to check the mail, would you find yourself checking over your shoulder in fear?

As happens so often, the grief and anger that the victims' families felt did not resolve after Mary was locked away, nor did the terms of her release heal any wounds. If anything, knowing that she was going about her own daily life unnoticed and unidentified made the families of both her victims feel bitter, as though they themselves were prisoners. Mary was free to work and raise her daughter out of the glare of the media spotlight, but the families did not have this same luxury.

Mary Flora Bell—whomever and wherever she is today—will forever be known as the little girl with the angelic face who killed two small boys. In 1968, it was a crime which was quite unheard of, especially in her small corner of the world; Newcastle on Tyne, England.

It is a tale of sadness and brutality, as well as one of redemption. Mary Bell was a child damaged by the abuse she suffered at home and damaged by the lack of love and nurturing every child needs to grow and become a well-adjusted individual. Mary had been hurt so utterly deeply, that it seems pain was the only thing she had to give others.

The objective of this book is not to excuse any of Mary's actions. Even most small children understand right from wrong, but in Mary's case, it is difficult at times to discern whether she understood right from wrong and simply chose to do wrong, or if she was truly incapable of understanding the difference.

By studying Mary's psychosocial background, crimes, and the punishment she received, we can possibly gain a better insight into what went wrong, if the punishment was sufficient to meet the crimes, and if the punishment appears to have been effective.

The End of **The Preview**

Visit us at **truecrimeseven.com** or **scan QR Code using your phone's camera app** to find more true crime books and other cool goodies.

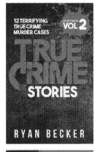

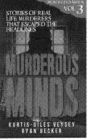

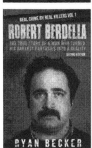
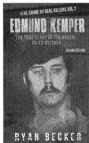
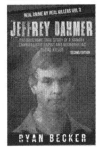

About True Crime Seven

True Crime Seven is about exploring the stories of the sinful minds in this world. From unknown murderers to well-known serial killers. It is our goal to create a place for true crime enthusiasts to satisfy their morbid curiosities while sparking new ones.

Our writers come from all walks of life but with one thing in common, and that is they are all true crime enthusiasts. You can learn more about them below:

Ryan Becker is a True Crime author who started his writing journey in late 2016. Like most of you, he loves to explore the process of how individuals turn their darkest fantasies into a reality. Ryan has always had a passion for storytelling. So, writing is the best output for him to combine his fascination with psychology and true crime. It is Ryan's goal for his readers to experience the full immersion with the dark reality of the world, just like how he used to in his younger days.

Nancy Alyssa Veysey is a writer and author of true crime books, including the bestselling, Mary Flora Bell: The Horrific True Story Behind an Innocent Girl Serial Killer. Her medical degree and work in the field of forensic psychology, along with postgraduate studies in criminal justice, criminology, and pre-law, allow her to bring a unique perspective to her writing.

Kurtis-Giles Veysey is a young writer who began his writing career in the fantasy genre. In late 2018, he parlayed his love and knowledge of history into writing nonfiction accounts of true crime stories that occurred in centuries past. Told from a historical perspective, Kurtis-Giles brings these victims and their killers back to life with vivid descriptions of these heinous crimes.

Kelly Gaines is a writer from Philadelphia. Her passion for storytelling began in childhood and carried into her college career. She received a B.A. in English from Saint Joseph's University in 2016, with a concentration in Writing Studies. Now part of the real world, Kelly enjoys comic books, history documentaries, and a good scary story. In her true-crime work, Kelly focuses on the motivations of the killers and backgrounds of the victims to draw a complete picture of each individual. She deeply enjoys writing for True Crime Seven and looks forward to bringing more spine-tingling tales to readers.

James Parker, the pen-name of a young writer from New Jersey, who started his writing journey with play-writing. He has always been fascinated with the psychology of murderers and how the media might play a role in their creation. James loves to constantly test out new styles and ideas in his writing so one day he can find something cool and unique to himself.

Brenda Brown is a writer and an illustrator-cartoonist. Her art can be found in books distributed both nationally and internationally. She has also written many books related to her graduate degree in psychology and her minor in history. Like many true crime enthusiasts, she loves exploring the minds of those who see the world as a playground for expressing the darker side of themselves—the side that people usually locked up and hid from scrutiny.

Genoveva Ortiz is a Los Angeles-based writer who began her career writing scary stories while still in college. After receiving a B.A. in English in 2018, she shifted her focus to nonfiction and the real-life horrors of crime and unsolved mysteries. Together with True Crime Seven, she is excited to further explore the world of true crime through a social justice perspective.

You can learn more about us and our writers at:

https://truecrimeseven.com/about/

For updates about new releases, as well as exclusive pro-
motions, join True Crime Seven readers' group and you can
also **receive a free book today.** Thank you and see you
soon.
Sign up at: **freebook.truecrimeseven.com/**

Or **scan QR Code using your phone's camera app.**

Dark Fantasies Turned Reality

Prepare yourself, we're not going to **hold back on details or
cut out any of the gruesome truths...**

Made in the USA
Columbia, SC
13 November 2022

71141311R00067